American Flag

Q&A

 Smithsonian |  Collins

An Imprint of HarperCollins Publishers

Smithsonian Mission Statement

For more than 160 years, the Smithsonian has remained true to its mission, "the increase and diffusion of knowledge." Today the Smithsonian is not only the world's largest provider of museum experiences supported by authoritative scholarship in science, history, and the arts but also an international leader in scientific research and exploration. The Smithsonian offers the world a picture of America, and America a picture of the world.

Special thanks to Jennifer L. Jones, Chair, Division of Military History and Diplomacy, National Museum of American History, Behring Center, Smithsonian Institution, for her invaluable contribution to this book.

Special thanks to Kathleen Kendrick, Project Curator, National Museum of American History, Behring Center, Smithsonian Institution, for her invaluable contribution to this book.

This book was created by **jacob packaged goods LLC** (www.jpgglobal.com).
Written by: Denise Rinaldo
Creative: Ellen Jacob, Sarah Thomson, Jeff Chandler, Andrea Curley, Louise Jacob

Photo and art credits: pages 2, 7 inset, 10, 13 (top, center left and right), 14, 17, 21, 22–23, 25, 26 (both), 31, 33, 43 inset: The Granger Collection, New York; **pages 11, 13 (bottom), 14 inset, 17 inset, 20, 25 inset, 33 inset, 34, 36:** © Jeff Chandler; **pages 35, 37 inset, 38–39:** APImages; **pages 3, 18–19:** Harry T. Peters Collection, National Museum of American History, Behring Center, Smithsonian Institution; **pages 28–29, 30–31:** Division of Military History and Diplomacy, National Museum of American History, Behring Center, Smithsonian Institution; **pages 6–7:** © Mark E. Gibson/Dembinsky Photo Associates; **page 8:** © Publiphoto/Photo Researchers, Inc.; **page 9:** © Rafael Macia/Photo Researchers, Inc.; **page 37:** © Dan Dempster/Dembinsky Photo Associates; **page 40:** © Joseph Sohm/Photo Researchers, Inc.; **page 43:** NASA; **page 45:** Hugh Talman/Smithsonian Institution photographer

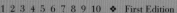

1 2 3 4 5 6 7 8 9 10 ◆ First Edition

Contents

What country do you think of when you see this flag?

When you saw those stars and stripes, one place probably flashed into your mind: the United States of America. The flag is a **symbol** of our country. When people see it, they are reminded of what this country means to them.

The flag is a symbol because it stands for something. The designs *on* the flag are symbols too. The thirteen stripes make us think of the thirteen **colonies** that joined together to form the United States. The fifty stars are for the fifty states in our country today.

Many people call the flag the "Stars and Stripes."

Flags can be symbols of countries, states, clubs, or even ideas. A white flag, for example, means "I surrender." But no matter what they stand for, there are some things that all flags have in common.

Canton—any quarter of the flag, but commonly the upper left quarter

Field—the background of the flag

This red and white maple leaf design became Canada's official flag on February 15, 1965.

Charge—an object or design on a flag's field

Hoist side—the side of the flag closest to the flagstaff

Flagstaff—the pole that supports the flag

Fly—the side of the flag that is farthest from the flagstaff

How are all flags alike?

Flags have been around for such a long time that a flag language has developed to describe them. A flag's field is its background. A pirate flag has a black field with a skull and crossbones at the center. A design such as the skull and crossbones is called a charge. The charge on a Canadian flag is a maple leaf.

Other parts of the flag include the hoist side, fly side, and canton. All flags have the same parts, but each country's flag is unique—different from any other country's.

Some countries change their flags over time. Others have had the same design for centuries.

Flags are some of the oldest symbols in the world.

A white skull and crossbones on a black field is called a Jolly Roger—a pirate flag.

Where did flags come from?

In China as well as in Rome, over 2,800 years ago, generals flew flags from chariots so that their soldiers would know when they were close by. The high-flying flag could be seen from farther away than the chariot itself. Later, in the Middle Ages in Europe, knights carried flags in battle so their friends could tell them from their enemies. (Everyone looks alike in armor!)

Battle flags helped people communicate when they were too far away to talk. Ships also began to fly flags that let people know which country they came from. National flags, such as the Stars and Stripes, developed from these. Today each country has its own flag, and looking at that flag can tell you about the country's history.

For centuries ships have sailed around the world to ports far from home. Sailors use flags to announce what country each ship is from.

SMITHSONIAN LINK
The Smithsonian has its own flag. Its charge is a sunburst symbolizing knowledge. See it here:
http://photo2.si.edu/150now/150bell.htm

These fifteenth-, sixteenth-, and seventeenth-century suits of armor—on display at the Metropolitan Museum of Art in New York City—show the flags that identified the knights during battle.

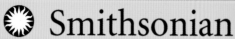
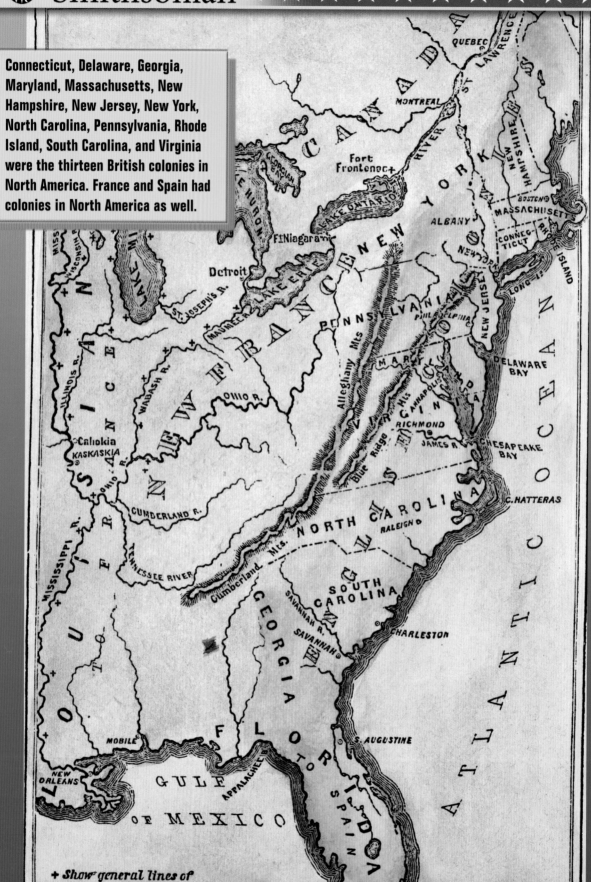

Connecticut, Delaware, Georgia, Maryland, Massachusetts, New Hampshire, New Jersey, New York, North Carolina, Pennsylvania, Rhode Island, South Carolina, and Virginia were the thirteen British colonies in North America. France and Spain had colonies in North America as well.

+ Show general lines of French military posts.

What were the first American flags?

Before the Revolutionary War, there was no such place as the United States of America. Along the east coast of what is now our country there were thirteen colonies. A colony is a settlement that's ruled by a far-off country. These thirteen colonies were ruled by the British. In fact, Great Britain ruled colonies all over the world. The flag that flew over every one of them was called the Union Jack.

In the 1760s some American colonists decided that they didn't want to be ruled by the British anymore. People started saying that maybe the colonies should form a new nation—separate from Great Britain. Some colonists began to make and fly flags to spread the idea that the colonies should be independent.

"Union Jack" is the nickname for Great Britain's flag. It was a union, or a combination, of two flags: a red cross for England and a white diagonal cross for Scotland. (Later a red diagonal cross, for Ireland, was added.)

What flags did the colonists fly?

The Revolutionary War started in 1775. Troops led by George Washington fought against the British until 1783. Then Americans finally won independence for their new country—the United States of America.

Before independence colonists used many different flags.

Some carried slogans such as "Liberty or Death" to show the colonists' anger with the way the British ruled them. Some flags had stripes, crosses, trees, and even rattlesnakes on them. Benjamin Franklin explained why the rattlesnake was a good symbol for the colonists: the rattlesnake doesn't attack unless it's threatened, it is fierce, and it doesn't back down.

Flags let the American colonists show others how they felt. When George Washington raised a flag over his army's camp, he wrote that he was saluting the "United Colonies." This flag declared how the colonists felt about one another—and about England too.

A rattlesnake, a symbol of independence, was used on this naval flag.

DONT TREAD ON ME

Many flags with pine trees, such as these two, were flown as symbols of the New England colonies.

AN APPEAL TO HEAVEN

This blue flag, called the Liberty Flag, was flown in the southern colonies during the Revolutionary War.

LIBERTY

George Washington flew the Grand Union flag near his army's camp at Prospect Hill in Massachusetts on New Year's Day, 1776.

What was the Grand Union flag?

The flag that Washington first raised over his camp was called the Grand Union. It had thirteen red and white stripes, a symbol of the thirteen colonies standing together against unfair British rules. But it also had something else—a Union Jack in the corner. Remember, the Union Jack was the *British* flag. Including it in the Grand Union flag showed that not all colonists were ready to break all ties with Great Britain.

Some still felt connected to the country that had governed them.

Some British soldiers who saw the Grand Union thought that Washington was flying the British flag as a sign of surrender. They were wrong. On July 4, 1776, the Americans declared independence from England.

Now the country needed a flag without the Union Jack.

A soldier holds the Grand Union flag as George Washington takes command of the colonial army on July 3, 1775.

What did the first Stars and Stripes look like?

In June 1777 a group of American leaders met in Philadelphia. At this meeting, they agreed on a new flag for their new country. It would have thirteen red and white stripes and thirteen white stars in a blue canton. The Union Jack was removed from the canton, and the Stars and Stripes was born.

Who actually cut out the stars and stripes and sewed them into a flag is a mystery. There is a famous story that a Philadelphia woman named Betsy Ross made the first American flag after George Washington showed her the design.

We don't know who sewed that first flag. And before the Stars and Stripes could fly over an independent country, there were still many battles to be fought.

SMITHSONIAN LINK
See some early American flag designs at:
www.americanhistory.si.edu/ssb/6_thestory/6c_stars/fs6c.html

British general John Burgoyne surrenders his army at Saratoga on October 17, 1777. It was the Americans' first great victory of the Revolutionary War.

Many paintings of the early Stars and Stripes show the stars in a circle. But most often the stars were in rows.

Did soldiers carry the new flag in battle?

The Stars and Stripes was not a battle flag. It was flown mainly over forts and camps. Even so, many people think Revolutionary War soldiers went into battle carrying the new American flag. That's partly the fault of a famous painting, *George Washington Crossing the Delaware*, by Emanuel Leutze. The huge canvas shows General Washington standing tall in a boat, the flag behind him, as soldiers row across a raging river.

Washington *did* lead his troops across the Delaware River to a great victory. But he

wouldn't have carried the national flag; and even if he had, it wouldn't have been the one shown in the painting. The crossing happened on Christmas Day, 1776—before the Stars and Stripes existed.

Even though Washington's rowboat didn't fly the Stars

The painting (which inspired this print) is famous—but the flag is wrong! George Washington would not have flown the Stars and Stripes as he crossed the Delaware River.

and Stripes, some other ships did. One of those ships was captained by a man named John Paul Jones.

What flag flew on John Paul Jones's ship?

On September 23, 1779, Captain John Paul Jones's ship was badly damaged in a fierce battle with the British ship *Serapis*. Jones's flag wound up floating in the sea. When the British captain saw that the American flag was no longer flying, he asked if Jones had surrendered. Jones boldly declared, "I have not yet begun to fight!"

Jones and his men fought their way aboard the *Serapis*, defeated the British, and took control of their ship. The *Serapis* now flew the American flag, the Stars and Stripes. But it was different from the flag we know today: it had blue, red, and white stripes, not just red and white ones.

This battle was only one of many in the Revolutionary War. It took eight long years of fighting before the Americans won their independence. And even then, a problem with the flag held up the victory celebrations.

The flag Jones flew on the *Serapis* had stripes in three colors, not just two. People were still trying to decide what the Stars and Stripes should look like.

SMITHSONIAN LINK
To see a portrait of John Paul Jones, visit:
www.americanhistory.si.edu/collections/navigation/jones.htm

This action-filled print shows John Paul Jones capturing the *Serapis*.

What happened to the flag in New York City?

After the United States, now an independent country, signed a peace treaty with England, George Washington led his army into New York City. The painter imagined the Stars and Stripes waving behind him.

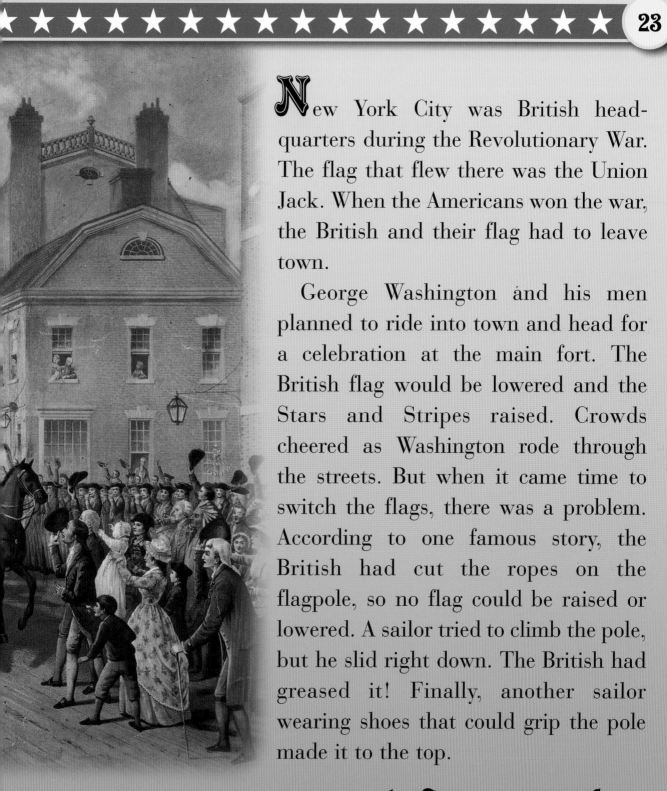

New York City was British head-quarters during the Revolutionary War. The flag that flew there was the Union Jack. When the Americans won the war, the British and their flag had to leave town.

George Washington and his men planned to ride into town and head for a celebration at the main fort. The British flag would be lowered and the Stars and Stripes raised. Crowds cheered as Washington rode through the streets. But when it came time to switch the flags, there was a problem. According to one famous story, the British had cut the ropes on the flagpole, so no flag could be raised or lowered. A sailor tried to climb the pole, but he slid right down. The British had greased it! Finally, another sailor wearing shoes that could grip the pole made it to the top.

At last the Stars and Stripes flew over a new nation.

What kind of flag flew over Fort McHenry?

The end of the Revolutionary War began almost thirty years of peace for the United States. But the British and Americans fought again in the War of 1812.

One battle took place at Fort McHenry, near the entrance to Baltimore's harbor. Before dawn, British warships began firing cannons at the fort. The bombardment went on for twenty-five hours straight—until dawn the following day.

The Americans in the fort fought back bravely. Finally they forced the British to give up.

At the end of the fight, the American commander ordered his men to raise an American flag. The flag was huge—thirty feet by forty-two feet. It had fifteen stripes and fifteen stars. But what really earned the Fort McHenry flag a place in American history was the song written about it.

Oh, say, can you see, by the dawn's early light, What so proudly we hail'd at the twilight's last gleaming? ...

A young lawyer named Francis Scott Key watched the battle of Fort McHenry from on board a ship, waiting to see who would win.

The flag flown at Fort McHenry had fifteen stars and fifteen stripes. The new stars and stripes stood for two new states, Vermont and Kentucky.

In 1814, an artist named John Bower created this image of British ships attacking Fort McHenry.

Key made several handwritten copies of his verses about the Fort McHenry battle. This one is from about 1840.

Why was the Fort McHenry flag called the Star-Spangled Banner?

The famous song about the Fort McHenry flag is none other than "The Star-Spangled Banner." Francis Scott Key watched the Fort McHenry battle from a ship. As dawn came, Key looked anxiously toward the fort. When he saw the flag flying, he knew the Americans had beaten their enemy. He began writing a poem that could be sung to the tune of a popular English song.

The song, with Key's new words, grew more and more popular. In 1931 Congress made it our national anthem. The flag that Key wrote about is now called the Star-Spangled Banner, and those words became a nickname for every U.S. flag. Another war and another flag created a new nickname for the flag—Old Glory.

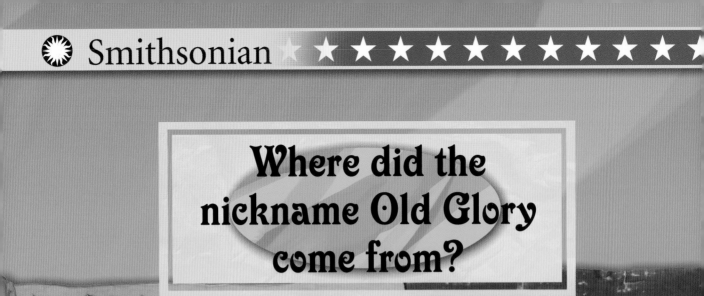

Where did the nickname Old Glory come from?

When Old Glory was first made, it had twenty-four stars. Later seven more stars were added, along with a white anchor that stood for the years William Driver and Old Glory spent sailing.

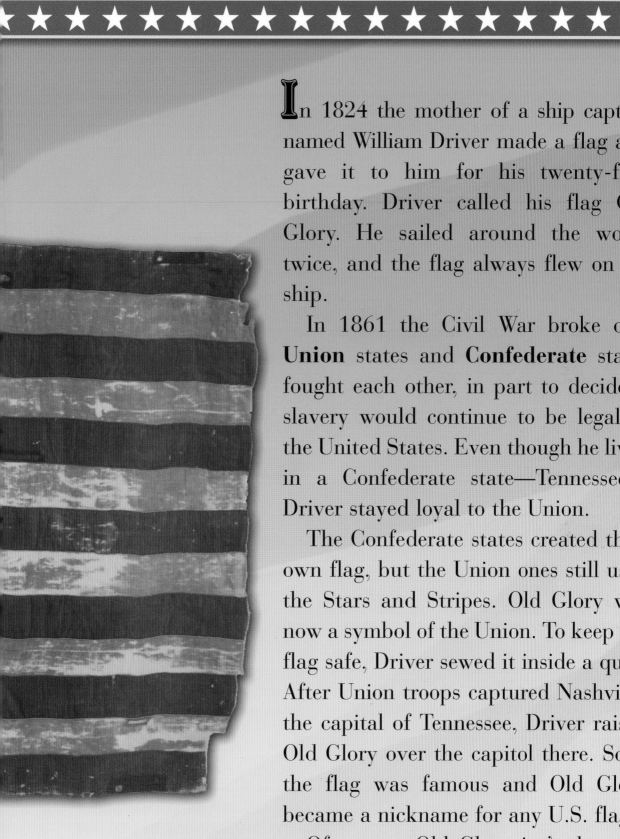

In 1824 the mother of a ship captain named William Driver made a flag and gave it to him for his twenty-first birthday. Driver called his flag Old Glory. He sailed around the world twice, and the flag always flew on his ship.

In 1861 the Civil War broke out. **Union** states and **Confederate** states fought each other, in part to decide if slavery would continue to be legal in the United States. Even though he lived in a Confederate state—Tennessee—Driver stayed loyal to the Union.

The Confederate states created their own flag, but the Union ones still used the Stars and Stripes. Old Glory was now a symbol of the Union. To keep the flag safe, Driver sewed it inside a quilt. After Union troops captured Nashville, the capital of Tennessee, Driver raised Old Glory over the capitol there. Soon the flag was famous and Old Glory became a nickname for any U.S. flag.

Of course, Old Glory isn't the only famous Civil War flag.

Why did Confederates have their own flags?

The Stars and Bars was the first Confederate flag. The eight stars stood for the first eight states that broke away from the country.

Eleven Southern states intended to split from the rest of the country and create the Confederate States of America. Of course, they wanted a flag. Leaders designed one known as the Stars and Bars.

This Confederate battle flag was captured at the battle of Gettysburg.

Since the Stars and Bars looked a lot like the Stars and Stripes, soldiers sometimes got confused.

So officers created a special battle flag. It was a symbol known as the Southern Cross—a blue *X* decorated with white stars—against a red background.

This battle flag became the basis of a new national flag for the Confederate states. It was white, with the battle flag as the canton. From certain angles it looked like a flag of surrender, so the Confederates came up with a fourth flag. But they hardly got a chance to use it, because the war was almost over.

SMITHSONIAN LINK
Check out a Confederate flag at
www.americanhistory.si.edu/militaryhistory/collection/object.asp?ID=193&back=1

Did the Union flag change during the Civil War?

President Abraham Lincoln wanted the country to stay together. As a symbol of that, he flew the Stars and Stripes over the White House during the Civil War. Some people wanted him to remove the stars that stood for the Confederate states. Lincoln said no. The flag he flew included stars for every American state—both Union and Confederate.

On April 14, 1865, President Lincoln was in a theater watching a play from a flag-draped box seat. John Wilkes Booth, an actor who sided with the Confederacy, entered the box and shot Lincoln. Booth then jumped from the box to the stage, but he caught his foot on flag-patterned **bunting**, fell, and broke his leg. He rode off on horseback; but the injury slowed him down, and government troops trapped him in a barn. In a way, the flag helped to catch the president's killer.

SMITHSONIAN LINK
See a thirty-five star flag used during the Civil War
at www.civilwar.si.edu/soldiering_84th_flag.html

John Wilkes Booth shot Abraham Lincoln on April 14, 1865. Friends of his were supposed to assassinate the vice president and the secretary of state as well. But the plan didn't work, and only Lincoln died.

In 1865, when President Lincoln was killed, the Stars and Stripes had thirty-six stars.

Delaware 1787
Pennsylvania 1787
New Jersey 1787
Georgia 1788
Connecticut 1788

Massachusetts 1788
Maryland 1788
South Carolina 1788
New Hampshire 1788
Virginia 1788

New York 1788
North Carolina 1789
Rhode Island 1790
Vermont 1791
Kentucky 1792

Tennessee 1796
Ohio 1803
Louisiana 1812
Indiana 1816
Mississippi 1817

Illinois 1818
Alabama 1819
Maine 1820
Missouri 1821
Arkansas 1836

Michigan 1837
Florida 1845
Texas 1845
Iowa 1846
Wisconsin 1848

California 1850
Minnesota 1858
Oregon 1859
Kansas 1861
West Virginia 1863

Nevada 1864
Nebraska 1867
Colorado 1876
North Dakota 1889
South Dakota 1889

Montana 1889
Washington 1889
Idaho 1890
Wyoming 1890
Utah 1896

Oklahoma 1907
New Mexico 1912
Arizona 1912
Alaska 1959
Hawaii 1959

How has the flag changed over the years?

Every time a new state joined the United States, a new star was added to the flag (on the 4th of July following its entrance into the Union). For a while, people thought it would be a good idea to have a stripe for each state too. But as the country grew, they changed their minds. In 1818 Congress passed a law saying that the flag would always have thirteen stripes—no more. The thirteen stripes would honor the thirteen original colonies.

On July 4, 1960, the forty-ninth and fiftieth stars (for Alaska and Hawaii) were added to the flag. A seventeen-year-old named Robert Heft designed a way to arrange the stars as a project for his high school history class. He got a B⁻ for the assignment. However, when he sent his flag to a congressman, who worked to get it accepted as the new national flag, his teacher changed his grade to an A!

Robert Heft's history project changed the flag forever. Another school assignment became a way to celebrate the flag's birthday—Flag Day.

Robert Heft, holding the fifty-star flag he designed.

What is Flag Day?

It is the day to celebrate the American flag. It is held on June 14, because on that day in 1777 the Stars and Stripes became the official flag of the United States.

Flag Day started out as a celebration on local levels in the 1870s, including a national observance of Flag Day on June 14, 1877, the centennial of the flag. In 1885 a teacher in Wisconsin had his students write essays answering the question "What does the flag mean to you?" After that the teacher, Bernard John Cigrand, wrote articles and made speeches encouraging Americans to fly flags and hold parades on June 14. In 1949 President Harry S. Truman signed an act of Congress making that day National Flag Day.

Flag Day is a good way to honor the flag and its history. Another U.S. holiday, Columbus Day, inspired something else connected with the flag—the Pledge of Allegiance.

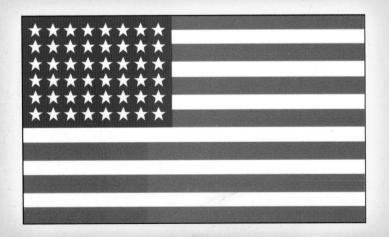

In 1949, when Flag Day became a holiday, the Stars and Stripes had forty-eight stars. Later two more stars, for Alaska and Hawaii, would be added to make the fifty-star flag we use today.

Flag Day lets everyone celebrate the Stars and Stripes. What can you do to show you're proud of the flag?

President Harry Truman signs the bill that made Flag Day a national holiday.

What is the Pledge of Allegiance?

All over the country, children learn to recite the thirty-one words of the pledge.

The **pledge** made its first appearance in September 1892 in a popular children's magazine called *The Youth's Companion*. The magazine called on kids across the country to recite the pledge on Columbus Day. By doing so they would promise **allegiance**—or loyalty—to the country for which the flag stands, the United States of America. After that it became a tradition (or a law, in some places) for students to say the pledge at the beginning of every school day.

When you say the Pledge of Allegiance, you stand facing the flag and put your right hand over your heart. And there are not only rules about the Pledge of Allegiance. There are rules about the flag too.

I pledge allegiance to the flag of the United States of America, and to the Republic for which it stands, one nation, under God, indivisible, with liberty and justice for all.

A ranger in a national park raises the flag. If you want to fly the flag, learn the Flag Code so that you can treat it with respect.

When and how should you fly the flag?

The U.S. Flag Code tells you everything you need to know about flying the flag and caring for it. The code was written by the U.S. Congress. Here are some of the rules. Following them shows that you respect the flag as a symbol of your country and its values.

• If you fly a flag outdoors, take it down at night unless there are lights set up to shine on it in the dark. If it's raining or snowing, take down your flag unless it's waterproof.

• When you **hoist** a flag, do it briskly. Lower it slowly and smoothly.

• Fly the flag upside down *only* to signal that you're in danger.

• Never let the flag touch the ground.

• Do not fly a flag that is torn, dirty, or worn out.

Wherever the American flag is flown, these rules should be followed. And the flag has been flown in some amazing places.

SMITHSONIAN LINK
Find out about rules for flying the flag here.
www.americanhistory.si.edu/ssb/6_thestory/6c_stars/fs6c.html

In what unexpected places has the flag been flown?

In 1969 American astronauts Buzz Aldrin and Neil Armstrong became the first humans to set foot on another world. Four days after launching, they landed on the moon and planted a three-by-five-foot nylon flag in the lunar soil.

The American flag flies in some remote places on Earth too. In 1962 climber Barry Bishop left a flag atop Mount Everest, the world's highest peak. Explorer Robert Peary made it to the North Pole in 1909 and left an American flag to prove it.

People fly flags not just on other worlds and in faraway lands but also in front of their homes, schools, stores, and more. You see the American flag in parades and in parks and in many other places. Wherever the Stars and Stripes flies, it is a symbol of American values: life, liberty, and the pursuit of happiness.

Neil Armstrong took this photo (right) of Buzz Aldrin and the Stars and Stripes they planted during the first manned mission to the moon.

SMITHSONIAN LINK
See the two flags that were exchanged when the United States and the Soviet Union cooperated in the first international space flight.
www.nasm.si.edu/exhibitions/attm/pa.3.html

This postcard celebrates Robert Peary's expedition to the North Pole in 1909.

Meet the Curator

Jennifer L. Jones
CHAIR, DIVISION OF MILITARY HISTORY
AND DIPLOMACY
**National Museum of American
History, Behring Center,
Smithsonian Institution**

Why did you become a curator and historian?

In my senior year in high school, a history teacher and a good friend from school made me think about history in a very different way—through historical objects—and I was hooked. Internships and many different exhibit projects have allowed me to research all different facets of history by learning about the objects, the people who made them, and what life was like when the objects were made.

How can kids get interested in your field?

Talk to your parents, grandparents, neighbors, and friends about what their lives were like as kids, what kinds of things they did—their personal history. As someone who is interested in military history and flags, I'd ask them if they flew flags on patriotic holidays, if anyone in the family was in the military, what life was like during a time in their life when we were at war, and then just listen. See if they have stuff from their experiences, and ask to see it.

What do you do every day?

No two days of my job are ever the same. I give tours and presentations, especially to high school history teachers, and sometimes do interviews about our collections and exhibitions. As a supervisor, I also have to manage the work of other curators. Sometimes I go to the library and get a book on the subject or check my sources, or sometimes I go into the collections' storage areas to look for an object we have that might be similar to their object.

Do you need any special training (apart from a college education) for your job?

I took a lot of extra history classes in high school. My mom was a U.S. history and English teacher, so my interest in history is thanks to her. I studied American history and U.S. literature in college, but it was through my internships here at the National Museum of American History that I was able to really learn about the "stuff" of history; the material culture, what people used and how they used it, really taught me about my field.

Digging through thousands of records may be tedious, but it is so exciting when you find the information you've been looking for. It's a lot like detective work, figuring out what something is or, just as often, what it is not. To be a curator, you have to learn to really look at objects, study them, feel them, and research them. Then you can understand them and put them into historical context.

What other experts do you consult to help you with your work?

I consult lots of different people: flag experts, conservators, military uniform experts, firearms experts. I also consult with staff from other areas of the museum—such as textile analysis, for flags and uniforms—that overlap with our collections.

What is the biggest surprise you have had in your own work?

I thing the biggest surprise in my work is that it has been so varied over the past twenty years. I started as an intern, then became a research assistant for a Japanese American history exhibit and developed a national collection of Japanese American internment materials. I've managed and curated many exhibits, including one featuring the objects that have been left at the Vietnam Veterans Memorial. I also helped to develop a major exhibit covering 250 years of America's military history, and selected many of the objects to be featured in collections associated with these exhibits.

What was the most exciting discovery you ever made?

One day, while looking for documents for a researcher, we found what appeared to be the hoist rope and sleeve that had been cut away from the hoist edge of the Star-Spangled Banner during its conservation treatment in 1914 by Amelia Fowler. It is now exhibited with the rest of the flag. Talk about a find!

Glossary

allegiance—Loyalty. Someone who pledges allegiance to a flag is promising to support and take care of the country for which the flag stands.

bunting—Long strips of cloth, often decorated with the colors or patterns of flags, that can be draped or hung as decoration.

colonies—territories or areas under the control of a far-off nation. The colonies that became the United States of America were under the control of Great Britain.

Confederacy—The alliance created by the Southern states that broke off from the United States in 1860 and 1861: the Confederate States of America (CSA). "Confederate" means an adherent to the CSA.

hoist—Lift. When you lift or raise a flag up a flagpole, you are hoisting it.

pledge—Promise.

regimental—To do with a regiment, which is a military fighting group. During the Revolutionary War, and in other wars as well, regiments had their own flags, which were called regimental flags.

symbol—Something that stands for something else, usually something that cannot be easily pictured. The American flag is a symbol of the United States of America.

Union—The northern and western states that remained part of the United States during the Civil War. Literally, a union is a combining of separate things into one. The United States is a single country created by the union of states.

More to See and Read

Websites

There are links to many wonderful web pages in this book. But the web is constantly growing and changing, so we cannot guarantee that the sites we recommend will be available. If the site you want is no longer there, you can always find your way to plenty of information about the American flag through the main Smithsonian website: www.si.edu.

Read the whole story of the Star-Spangled Banner and how it is being preserved by experts at the Smithsonian Institution: http://americanhistory.si.edu/ssb

Find answers to all your questions about how to respect and care for the flag, including a full copy of the U.S. Flag Code: www.legion.org/?section=americanism

See flags from every country in the world and find out what their symbols mean: www.countryreports.org/flags/nationalflags.aspx

Suggested Reading

I Pledge Allegiance by Bill Martin, Jr., and Michael Sampson, illustrated by Chris Raschka. The pledge, its history, and what it means to different people.

Firefly Guide to Flags of the World. A look at other countries' flags.

Hold the Flag High by Catherine Clinton, illustrated by Shane W. Evans. The true story of how William Carney—the first African American to win the Congressional Medal of Honor—fought bravely and saved the flag during a Civil War battle.

The American Revolution for Kids: A History with 21 Activities by Janis Herbert. All about the war that made the American flag possible and what life was like in those days.

Let It Begin Here! Lexington and Concord: First Battles of the American Revolution by Dennis Brindell Fradin, illustrated by Larry Day. A dramatic, close-up look at the early battles in the War for Independence.

Index

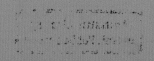